THE CROWD INSIDE

THE CROWD INSIDE

Elizabeth Libbey

Carnegie-Mellon University Press
Pittsburgh & London 1978

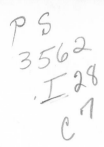

for my mother and father

Acknowledgments

American Poetry Review: "Bloodline: Grandmother Elander," "To Her Dead Mate: Montana, 1966"; *The American Review:* "Concerning the Dead Women: the Munitions Plant Explosion: June, 1918"; *Another Chicago Magazine:* "Ceremonious," "Horses to Keep"; *Black Warrior Review:* "Building My Home in the Woods," "Insomnia: A Practical Guide," "Beyond Hearing, to be Asked In," "The Lie"; *Creel:* "Good Night"; *Epoch:* "Coming Back from the Cliff," "On Being Asked to Bring a Poem Back from Montana"; *Field:* "The Peninsula is Open 24 Hours a Day"; *The Iowa Review:* "How She Can Sing"; *Mati:* "Virginia Woolf: Journal from the Country"; *Montana Gothic:* " 'Something Old' "; *The New Yorker:* "A Happy Survival," "On Making His Bed One Morning," "Come into the Night Grove," "Participant"; *Out There:* "The Tragic Experience, Abridged," "She Wants to Love the Man," "The Musician," "Helpmate"; *Poetry:* "The Gesture," "Putting Things By," "Love Poem"; *Poetry Northwest:* "The Protagonist Visits the Funhouse"; *Seneca Review:* "An Impossible Couch to Rest On," "Not Words"; *Shenandoah:* "The Only Port in Montana"; *Three Rivers Poetry Journal:* "Forcing the End," "Da Vinci's Flying Machine," "Keeper"; *The American Poetry Anthology:* "Before the Mountain," "Marceline, to Her Husband"; *Where We Are: An Anthology of Montana Poets:* "Hand Hold."

"How She Can Sing" first appeared in *The Iowa Review*, Volume 5, Number 1, Copyright © 1974 by the University of Iowa. "The Only Port in Montana" copyright © 1973 by Washington and Lee University, reprinted from *Shenandoah:* The Washington and Lee University Review with the permission of the editor. The following poems appeared originally in *The New Yorker: A Happy Survival* (1974), *On Making His Bed One Morning* (1977), *Participant*, and *Come Into The Night Grove* (1978); copyrighted © in the respective years shown, by The New Yorker Magazine, Inc.

In addition to the people whose names appear on these poems, thank you to Kris Bixby, Marvin Bell, Walter Brown, Tony Chanaka, Harry Hild, Laura Lovall, and Pamela Painter Skeen.

The publication of this book is supported by grants from the National Endowment for the Arts in Washington, D.C., a Federal agency, and from the Pennsylvania Council on the Arts.

Table of Contents

I. CEREMONIOUS

". . . within a single body
Heat fought with cold, wet fought with dry, the hard
Fought with the soft, things having weight contended
With weightless things."
    —Ovid, *Metamorphoses, Bk. I*
    (translation by Rolfe Humphries)

"Out of this same light, out of the central mind,
We make a dwelling in the evening air,
In which being there together is enough."
    —"Final Soliloquy of the Interior Paramour"
    —Wallace Stevens

CEREMONIOUS

"First—Chill—then Stupor—then the letting go—"
　　　　　　　　　—Emily Dickinson

If the nerves have betrayed, you'll always
have them your most demanding part.
They understand how you offer yourself,
how you want presents, how you won't
look into the hard glass, having yourself become
the quick blur of breath that freezes you.

And the crowd inside you
disperses, only the most curious
parts of yourself stay on, blinking
as if you're the flapping light, the turning
to somewhere from somewhere, someone made up.

A woman with no coat, walking her dog.
Let us rush into the very nerve that lulls her.
Let's walk with her off the curb.

MARCELINE, TO HER HUSBAND

"Yet I realized . . . how much
she needed my love, and I
enveloped her within it,
pretending the need was mine."
  —Andre Gide, *The Immoralist*

I'm yours, dearest, as are the winter towns,
their heady wines and soups.
My lungs fill. You bloom
in this air's thinness, a sudden crack
of ice or larches rushing at us across the lake.
Snow spattering your mouth. Landmarks:
like history, you need them.
Then, now, next month—always
the return to rooms in the evening,
hearing far off the harness bells, noticing
how our shadows race up the wooded slope.

How kind you are,
and god how your eyes go through me
as if I were the infection itself: unbearable
unless viewed as winter landscape.
This evening, I'll drink your wild face,
though that sad wine slide from my mouth.
Let me offer you my handkerchief, let me
toss this dark red luxury in your lap.
The harness bells, you say: harsh, perfect,
consummate. And this transparent snow . . .
my furs grow stiff around my shoulders.

for Linda Orr

CONCERNING THE DEAD WOMEN: THE
MUNITIONS PLANT EXPLOSION: JUNE, 1918.

What was most striking about them:
the absence of the expected long hair.
We sorted out blond brunette red gray black
and matched them as best we could
to the swelling complexions darkening in the heat, yet
not unpleasant to touch.

On the pleasant (though dusty) return to Milan,
we agreed we'd been saved
from the horror of such a disaster,
by that hair floating out from the barbed fence.
Bright as scarves, I remember.

As for those five or six who live on
long after metal has entered the brain: though the lieutenant
told us, Leave them alone, I and the corporal
cut off their heads. I won't soon forget my friend
poised above the girl with no face.

We agreed it was best
not to leave them breathing among the dead
in the wide soft trenches we made for them, saving
only the ribbons.

PARTICIPANT

You wait for something to happen.
Your breath is so many ice petals
dropped to the floor.
Watch out, even now
a tune deepens the erosive air,
even now the sinewy dancer
wakes and unfolds from his chair.
Your breath dances
with his, your mouth is his.
Only then does he whisper
what you want most
not to hear: you must not inhale
him so, there is no more room
for breath, let it
stand in your throat like so much
loose change. You wait, and
how brutally the dance continues.
How brutally
nothing is asked of you.

LEDA IN THE SUBURBS

Arms folded at the window, she
regards the garden
settled inside its frame
like a pastoral painting. Everything
grows toward her. And
there alone (the husband not home, the
children not born), she
mistakes herself for the sun.

The flat mask of dusk
deepens her breathing, there is
something more to
tonight's coming. The meaning
is not clear, yet she feels
significant as a star.
She wants to drift like evening itself.

There
by the back fence (does she
imagine it?) she stands waiting.
Night, like some black swan,
gathers at her shoulders,
forces her
down and open like any
ripe thing.

DA VINCI'S FLYING MACHINE

Before you know, the landscape is gone
and you watch yourself spin
away over water, thinking sea light that transforms you
is proper light for a pain worth remembering,
a pain that saves you. Long back,
who pulled you slippery from the sea?
Fish newly in flight in your jaws
are a wonderful face
you want to return to. The waves
slow for you in that special light
you dream of, dream you live new,
breaking the horizon.

for Richard Hugo

KEEPER

Uncle's fists curl on the globe
and won't let go. He recites
a poem in stiff German,
his voice giving
by degrees.
The boat inside my eyes
waltzes some mystic river.
Rain pours off the gutters.
"Someone is knocking, Uncle, someone
is trying to get in."

Uncle explains
the Universe to me again:
how orderly, how
exacting.
Planets career
about my head, in my pillow I try
to bury this hungry
skin of Venus.

Someone
is trying . . .
Uncle unfolds his violin
from its alligator case.
Water tumbles through me like some
close, ordinary beast.
In my sleep Uncle holds
a mirror to my mouth. "Breathe,"
he says
"slowly, slowly,"
to remind me.

PUTTING THINGS BY

Cutting plums, he hums until
the hum fills our heads.

His stories:
"Foxes, foxes in the grass,"
his hands like vines gone wild
against the wall. In perfect grass
the wicker chair blossoms.

Or
"Love and be loved. Think of that,"
he nods.

Digging roots this afternoon,
his hands were hard
tools. Hard as ice, air.
Gardenlike, is

the year a day?
I forget the important stories,
my hands are not his hands except
as the deep cut in the palm
hardens into rib.

Love and be loved. The year
is today. He seals the lids
tight to last.
He wants

things to be as they are.
They are.

for Bill Boggs

COMING BACK FROM THE CLIFF

His voice disappears inside her.
She is hollow.
Below her, the soapy gray eyes
of canyon rocks. His eyes among the eyes.
Suppose the clear lake is not the bottom; suppose
another cliff to follow down, and
never the lake. Walking back without him,
she sees him in the leaves, balanced
on the points of blue needles.
Still clinging in her throat.

BEFORE THE MOUNTAIN

Father, I expect your eyes
to regard me as lost. It is my
own eyes which surprise me.
Gone out of me, they watch
the mountain dusk
where you are, so approachable
in your disappearance.
How patient, the arc
of your red flare erasing itself.

Evening being sentimental, I wander
among the photos in their
metal frames. Not a life, but so close
to what a life seems: father and daughter
on the rock wall, tied waist to waist.
And this one shows candles
we placed, below zero, at the heads and feet
of the dead ones so the dead
wouldn't freeze.

Through the dark, your hand
waves at someone behind me, frozen
like wildflowers that amaze me
the way they curl out of the ice
at 10,000 feet. Father,
have you, unrescued,
exchanged gifts with the dark?
Am I your formal paying of respects
to night and snow, to rock?
You never named the gift I am. In your
photograph of no survivors, I'm smiling.

THE LIE

Alone in your room it's easy
to touch the soft skin of meaning.
Love seems promising.
You sneak inside the landscape
of words you trust.

You dance
into the arms of no one and somehow
don't fall. You convince the flutes
that you, not they, can dance.
And when those partners of the long lie collapse,
you simply whirl away.

Round the lighthouse, gliding out to sea,
you are a bird, graceful,
extracting itself from the landscape.
You get by
on languages you don't know,
you translate old friends
into a skin you think can hold you.
You want the lie to be your life.

II. SOMETHING OLD

BLOODLINE: GRANDMOTHER ELANDER

She sits in the garden chair.
Father hoses down
the patio, Mother in the pansies, bent.
And she sits in the garden, there,
the bean stalks waver
as she rises, moves through them.
The shadow of the oak moves to its base.
See her, how she arranges herself
under the oak for everyone,
how her wedding band
slides to the middle knuckle? Mine.

THINGS I KNOW OF YOU,
GRANDMOTHER BOGGS

I've been reading. You have
died in my absence.
Mother stands at the foot of your bed,
her head tilted: soft grey planet.
Father looks at your antique chairs,
counts them very
carefully.

I move forward in the room, scattering
long shadows of 5 p.m. My skin
irritates the air above your face.
I embrace
what isn't there, embrace you to
the smell of cabbage boiling, cabbage you refused
to dig up this morning.

You are looking hard
at the space between my eyes.
I've read some book which says
you may be drifting gently, bumping
like a balloon against the bedroom ceiling.
Interested in what
the Living have to say after the fact.

The fact is, little
has changed: just some life we don't

know about has moved in.
I decide against saying, Sorry.
You know better than that, you
who have always brushed words aside
as if they were starched lace
curtains you hated.
What is different
is this: your room
grown large around you. Unusable.

"SOMETHING OLD"

The feast is over.
I hear him downstairs with Father, he laughs,
at last let in on the joke
about Mother: her cold belly
in the dark thirty years. She stayed
for her glass of champagne, and wished us
the world, the many children of happiness.

What will he think
of my limbs locked in to Mother's
dream of grandchildren? He'll roll
out of me into sleep, something wild
hunting from water to water.
Father will tremble.

INSOMNIA: A PRACTICAL GUIDE

He rolls on his side and plays dead, but he's
making love to his dream in your bed.
Who built this house? You divide
the property, but it won't come out even,
so you listen
to the rattling trees, to potted plants
that wilt on the sill. He never
liked your garden.

That open sky drops down to meet you
until you realize
you can't stop the dream he's running away in:
it's his. The garden is his mother's.
A green thumb makes no difference: things come
to your window to die. Isn't that why
he's curling up slowly beside you? Isn't that
why he grows stale?

GOOD NIGHT

Animals defend me, then
the moon comes out. Grandmother Clock,
Grandfather Rocking Chair, and lilacs
from my husband. I'm plush, made
for furniture, and thinking apples, candies.

I think myself into degrees of things:
lie, view, rainbow. Waking
into something smaller than what I
slept to. My arm dangles from the bed,
survivor in shallow water.

Animals when I was young,
stayed animals, kept monsters caged
under the bed.
Monster, so comic and affectionate, please
make faces at my eyes closed too tightly,
my curled body.

Monster, ticking softly
inside me, I stare out from your
huge eyes, not knowing
the power days have: holding me,
they go under.

ON MAKING HIS BED ONE MORNING

I've considered light.
I like better looking into the dark.
Absence surrounds your glitter, Big Bear.
We're regular little planets
watching each other spin
and harden.

Next time
let's refuse what we can't break out of,
or outlive. Weren't my
mother, grandmothers, aunts,
happy brides?

Grandmother,
wanting someone to turn up the heat,
rose last night, and flapped her way
out of the blackness in me.

HELPMATE

after "Love Song: I and Thou" by Alan Dugan

Love, float into me for sleep's sake.
You're the body, the future.
I'm the house. Let's
put away the tools we used
for nailing down the marriage.
The bed might have looked better
hung on the wall.
Nothing would have worked out.

I love the neighborhood, the bureau drawers.
I love the care of the children,
the folding and putting away, the care
with which the children
say good night gently, go to their cars, and speed away.

Even if the home collapses
it is too well-practiced to fail for sure.
There will be no way to tell.

THE ONLY PORT IN MONTANA

That sailor I love is a cowboy
and he sailed over the edge
like a champion, tying knots around his neck.
I was a gift for anyone, having only
my rusty series of crawl, sidestroke,
and dead man's float,
to delay this strange sinking feeling.

Don't worry: I'm more careful of tide,
and I listen now to sea lions out on that rock
which looks like the boulder
I swore my love in the shadow of
in Lolo, Montana . . .
when they speak (the lions) they say
the last ship is gone
and will wash up somewhere, a much-needed
message for the world.

What worries me: that cowboy's
on board and heading West
to join his friends at the rodeo.
If I show up, Rodeo Queen on a stallion,
he'll still recognize my dock walk.

TO HER DEAD MATE: MONTANA, 1966

Hanged man, please grow wild and luminous
like these lanterns I hang from the aspens
to light your way. The moon won't
fall here because of you,
but moves off in the dark like horses.
My body feels empty
as reed pipes at the river. When they
speak they whistle. I'll
gather them to break your dead man's fall.

We should have been your mother's couple
at the seashore, not touching.
Admiring fog and pointing
away from here. So. They took
their last horse back. I want
to wrap you in my long skirt, carry you
until you are tall grass.

Husband, learn to dance
on this hushed wind: openness, the gray mouth
of your brain. Never let go.
Once under, you must
call yourself to yourself for keeps.

The dirt fills me
with its taste. And isn't it worth it? Listen:
the river, like riders, approaches from nowhere.

ON BEING ASKED TO BRING A POEM BACK FROM MONTANA

I sit underneath this cedar
thinking how you might see the river.
How the rocks glitter
green, how trout
lie easy in rock-shadow. Slow and
ripe. I cannot
catch a poem like that; carry it back,
a gift for your table.
No matter how fast I travel
down toward bottom, I miss, so I never
enter the water. Instead, I write
about mountains that ride the surface
toward me.

Did you know
tired Frenchmen first saw
Les trois tetons, called them
great breasts
rising hard under the touch of eyes?
How simple
it was. Like heat at noon. Insects
ticking
in the underbrush. Those trappers hunched
down against their horses' spines.
No sleep.

I've been dozing underneath
this cedar. While I dreamed it shifted, it
pulled itself away. Roots big as trees
tore themselves loose to make way for me.
I curl

into my burrow, imagining the perfect fit,
wondering if
I should mention the mountains again: how
Indians must have seen them first, left them
nameless, wandering off into the sun
just like water can.

I've wandered.
I want to say, See
this woman carrying her sagged breasts before her?
She and I don't need
to see our face in the water or on stone: we know
the bones in the cheeks fall
like eyes too long held steady against relentless sun.
This gift from the great West
is simply flat earth, flat sky. Nothing
in between horizons. No poem
to keep us from dying out here.

FORCING THE END

This story has been going on so long,
I want now
to turn the page until

I'm a girl in her swing,
pushed higher, swung out, tucked
at the knees, forcing
the rafters of her house to collapse.

On her face the lips
don't move: some things are told
by breathing.
While you sleep, she just keeps
swinging. There's no
star, no deep water
she's welcome to.

THE GESTURE

"In every parting there comes a moment when
the beloved is already no longer with us."
   —*Sentimental Education*
   —Gustave Flaubert

He leans forward in his chair.
She gazes
over the rim of her wine glass, at the candle
unlit between them.
From the formal red earth of the tablecloth,
a continent begins to spread itself:
the arrivals and departures
in separate airports, the sumptuous bars
they will visit, each
without the other. That darkness which
fills the room one shares
with a stranger, darkness more inclusive
than sleep.

It has been a long trip
into and out of that closeness
which softens the set of face, softens
even that withdrawal of hands
into themselves. There is
nothing to say. And yet, as the waiter
refolds his towel
deftly over his arm as a sign to begin,

those delicious possibilities
sweeten each small
gesture of goodbye. Each anonymous, misplaced smile.

For him
she will leave her spectacles folded
in her lap, she will smooth
her speckled hair, and drink
whatever he chooses.
For her
he will look upon that face as if
it were not growing indistinct. He will order
for them both, with usual aplomb,
the specialty of the house.
He will request
that the candle be lit.

III. THE PROTAGONIST VISITS THE FUNHOUSE

THE PROTAGONIST VISITS THE FUNHOUSE

I hear from the doctor the two of you
sat, shoulders closed,
on your bench under the oak (was it
those blackbirds swooping, offering food,
that frightened you? What to do with them.)

You think the doctor your insolent lover.
You, dressed newly in white.
He's faithful all right, he will
show you hanging moss and the watery enclosure.
Everything you're accustomed to.
You'll be expected
to take his arm for hunger.

Fold your head and tuck it away.
Confess: you long for the ticket
the attendant is selling at the entrance
to your doctor's good bed.
You're the bride, but what kind?
That beak you wear in your breast like a flower
reminds you, still life.

And it reminds you
of the open upturned throats. That your face
looks better on someone else,
that walking on the grounds all day
won't prevent your being extinct.

The doctor will teach you
to ride full dress and veil, sabre drawn,
but until you know who you're saving, stop galloping
down the corridor after no one toward the fence.
In the swamp, don't you know
the long-necked birds you love are choking?

VIRGINIA WOOLF: JOURNAL FROM THE COUNTRY

This morning the airplanes again:
little flashes above us
when we stand on the lawn after breakfast.
They are the Battle of Britain
staged for our household: a bomb
through the river's bank, water
breaking on the orchard.
Silenced, we walk
quickly to the house as if it could
protect us.

All this history to quiet us: London,
the disappearance of streets, disappearance
of what I know and do not know.
My collected years.
I am the woman pictured
on a garden bench, wicker hat drawn tight,
gaze secret. In London a woman sells flowers
and chants her incomprehensible song.
I follow her as I would follow water, she is
the revolving of my blood
when I walk quickly up and down the beach.

If it were not The War, I might
take my lamp and walk tonight to the river.
It is warm there, the water is warm,
very clear. Sky, very clear.
L. has pulled the black curtains. I must not
think whether things will come right.
The river is exemplary
among its apple trees. Dear L., dear river?,
there are things I do not know to write,
things I will not know. There is
an absence as if wind were missing by the ocean.
I cannot know, have I
written those voices truly as they speak?

THE PENINSULA IS OPEN 24 HOURS A DAY

I'm speaking of your heart:
late November. Your father's dog, gone mad,
shoots ahead on the cracked lake.
You aim. His legs trail out like filament.
You want to take
a loaf of snow in your hands, press snow
to his shagged throat. His trail
goes clear to the horizon, impossible
to follow. As you skate away,
you imagine him your father down and frozen.

And you remember your father
marching you into the snow, how he
tucked the cuffs of your trousers and offered
you his face. How could you refuse?
His face like terrible water rumbling
still wakes you.
The low ceiling floats, you under its ice,
and Father smiling down
through his open throat. You long to be
that anonymous shape
in stories you've read, that shape sealed
in the ice between water and air.
You long to watch yourself
on metal skates, part of a storybook
Father never understood. Smiling down
you slide over his face.

for Norman Dubie

CANCELLATION

Half-asleep I call you up,
breathing the number to myself, breathing hard.
I fear your anger, fear
you won't be angry.
I listen to the raw whir of kitchen clock,
to sun spreading
its grainy petulant gold against the window.

"I've overslept."
Or should I say,
"I've failed you, myself, deserve to be strung up, or
worse, abandoned to my own
sleep."
I apologize to please, apologize for
not knowing how to be there.
"We all make mistakes sometimes," you say, and
there isn't even the softest blade
buried in your voice.

I think to ask you how it ended, the dream
I dreamed you had. Did you
wander from room to room, gazing on mute green plants,
did you envision exotic blossoms
pushing through gray snow?
Or rather did you
think to go back forever, farther
than vision, thought—cool and safe
beneath the sheet, far asleep?
But I do not ask.

We discuss schedules, the possibility
of new appointments. You will call.
I wait, trying to hold
your voice, I wait
for something inside me to wake—some trust
to melt this rock-hard
understanding of myself. But fear
teaches me the next fear. I say only
what I know already: "goodbye."

THE EXILE

"And even from here I can hear—
Isn't this a miracle!—
The sounds of my own voice!"
    —"A Poem Without A Hero"
        —Anna Akhmathova

I am a photograph of myself
on the platform, dressed sensibly as if
I really mean to take the train.
Sparrows settle beside me,
not knowing I'm here I stand so motionless.
How easily I might open my fist, let
crumbs of nothing sprinkle
to the rumpled snow. How easily fooled,
like these sparrows, I might be.

But I've learned the light
ready to crack trying to hold things up.
The sparrows rise heavily,
crackling their iced wings, while I
stand frozen without regret, believing
in pure soft falling, the waiting, this
vast land shed of people. I've learned
if I move I must leave my last best strength behind.

Sometimes I think I've already leapt to the train,
travelled out past everything.
In the window, my face

clears itself of the gray uniform, doubt.
I concentrate, don't let
the train go slower than my hurtling shoulders.

But there's no train, my heart.
I stand here, wrapped about you, living ice.
Time may put this exile to sleep,
and so I woo sleep even as I taste air.
See? I stand, and here the casual sparrows
gathering along my arms. Do not
carve a name on me, or a set of years.
I don't breathe, but only for fear
the rising, the fall of my breasts
will give me away.

HORSES TO KEEP

Those horses
standing in the field across
from your house:
I don't
ride them, from here
they look like snow
gathering.

Someone
will rescue me—a rider,
snow. I'll
rescue you, be something
outside your window, something
you think you've lost.

While you sleep
in the false dark of curtains,
I'll arrange
your bones to fit your skin
perfectly, I'll
walk you anywhere
though there is rain, people—so
many excuses, no, this time

I'll stare at your face
until rain
asks us in, until this landscape
arrives or
leaves instead of doing
nothing.
We prod it

with a long stick, we walk
around the block.
The landscape
doesn't ask us in.
Only those horses
are a way to enter.

The light from my lantern
swings out to the houses, back
to horses, you're
among them, just when
I thought we were lost.
Running toward
you, I'm catching up
with myself.

for Peter Sears

THE MUSICIAN

The man at the piano
isn't playing it. In the next
room, his guests
laugh at the story he's told,
excusing himself, closing
the door between,
and since he can't see them
they are small hills on the prairie,
their laughter is water
he bends to, not drinking.
Smoothing it with his hand.

The guests rush in applauding
the story they take with them,
having become it.
They marvel
on the way to their cars, at his
practical smile. He smiles
good night
for his hands which, poised,
haven't begun to lower.

for Donald Justice

A HAPPY SURVIVAL

She breaks the best fan shell
into 14 razor slivers for 14 mornings
she will cut the ice from her legs, cut away
the warm shadow under each arm.
She will learn
what else can go: her deep fish-shadow
when she swims. Later the dry, hard shadow
wild salmon rise to. They
follow her as she follows the river.

"Old Interior," "Harm's Petal." She names
the river's arms. She sweats them out
to where the interior ends, sudden
as a map edge. Each elbow of river
could be anywhere;
she and the river close enough
to be mistaken for a single animal.

"Hello, night," she says.
She bends herself until she is a cup; she wants
to catch a surprise: her night shadow.
She wants to be a name made up. An exploration.
She looks down into her hand; she waits.
She must hear
the night there as it comes out of hiding; the chewing sound
night water makes.

for Deirdre Boggs

NOT WORDS

How amenable you are! You curve
into dark streets, waving affectionately.
To faces that hold you like touch
when the light is off, don't
be loving. Be civil.
In the name of acceptance wear
love's special occasion like a ring;
bless the wedding, legacy, apology,
time-of-day faces, and grow more fond
of each descent into hell, believing
each going from palace to palace
hasn't been ordinary.

Men love your romantic sadness; your understanding
of water. Nights caressing you.
They smile to think you walk sternly
for possession of yourself, walk late to know
the face of the town without them.
May you learn spaces between breath
are more relevant than a kiss. Plants want
sun, not words. You can't live like them,
wanting as you do, someone
to sit with you saying, I see now,
someone to say No to all the cozy
forgivenesses by a window.

You sway fondly through the world,

believing long-awaited arrivals present themselves
on the doorstep at last. Clouds build
and you wear them, smiling
as thunder rolls in. You, unpretentious
as rising water, make me believe
that falling together with someone
like rain in a dark field, means I see now,
that walking the long way back to a kiss
means love can be carried unbroken to the end.

for Tess Gallagher

THE TRAGIC EXPERIENCE, ABRIDGED

My luck is returning: I've found
a backwater tavern where old salts
tell their stories, harpooning the air.
They frown and nod with concern when I tell them
we've no legs for our rough line of work:
walking away from shipwrecks that never occur.
They say Learn to swim, be
an audience for sharks. Anything works.

Surely I'm big enough
to live off myself. Soon wind must come round
to my way of thinking . . . one thing
bothers me: a wind arrived last night.
No one knows where it came from, but it wants
to live here. It pushes my friends
into the sea. I've done all I can, haven't I?
I drink, I call them tragic and tourist, I tell them
there's no balmy South Pacific.

Me, I like this port,
its tough crafts bobbing on high water
like survivors dancing in the wreck
of that ship I'd jump
someday for sure. Wish you were here.
I carry your words in my pocket
when I walk to the point. I imagine you
calling a long way over the water.

for Walter King

IV.   HOW SHE CAN SING

HOW SHE CAN SING

Here he is, here is this situation: love.
The gravy, the cream, something fatter
than silence. The house shakes,
walls go, even the lamp she uses for heat,
huddling underneath it until morning.

Here is everything. In order, in a package.
She is a body again, a dull ticking
enters her skin. He is sudden
and pressing. He notices everything, arranges
everything. Cups fall into place,
the scratchings inside the wall grow quiet.

And even if he doesn't say
he will be back, he will be back.
Now nothing but the back of his head
disappearing. Outside, nothing is clear.
The sidewalks are damp, early,
the houses are the same.
He is the back of a face, his skin
is the past.

She feels herself circling him
wider and wider. She could
haul him in, she can let him go.
She looks at the window. It is her face,
she closes it. This is her hand
switching him off. She never needed this love,
she saw how it would be, knew
what he wanted. Looking back, she knows
how it will be. She enters it,
she sleeps. She always does.

SHE WANTS TO LOVE THE MAN

whose body is incorrect, but beautiful.
She wants to stop pretending.
Walking with a friend, she loves
how one side of his face becomes
another and another in the streetlights,
and each face more what she can live with
than the one before. Beside him,
not touching, she understands
his skin, his life, the way
he loses his hands to the quiet air.

She speaks to him, something
to a friend who loves her past as she does.
She mistakes his past for hers, mistakes
his silence for gesture, "Look
at the fireflies caught in warm air."

She thinks of him, tired, driving home
when he might have stayed, and of
the soft disappointment in his face, he
didn't want to stay. In the mirror
her breasts slope toward sleep.
Her body dreams
flawless ladies, flawless gentlemen,
sighing sleep, dancing sleep, kissing sleep.

INTRUSION

No You or I is to enter this poem.
Only landscape, cut briefly
by the idea We. The bird
passes across the field and disappears
observed by no one.

No window offers a view,
no clock circles, no one returns.
The sky says nothing
wild, peaceful, promises nothing
to feel at home in.

And if a pocket of sky becomes an
eye, a mouth, it is only We
determined to find a stone out of place,
to write, "They picked it up and
carried it together back to the sea."

Here amid blind wheat
the You, the I plan where
the window might best be.

We plan birds, all sorts, beating
their wings against the glass.

BUILDING MY HOME IN THE WOODS

on my arrival in a new town

"Why have you come here?" you ask
and offer me a pear. Outside, the trees
are fairly well, they flow along
like the river, like this conversation.
My home isn't here
or anywhere I've been. I want to raise
cucumbers in British Columbia,

I want to stir
plums and sugar in a huge iron pot
then set the sealed jars
on shelves I've built myself, shelves
I haven't built
for a husband's car keys, house key, cigarettes and
comb.

I suspect this is a nice enough town
once it snows,
but what do you do with your hands?
Besides: I'm not looking
for someone particular . . . I like the way you
ask me why I've come.

ENOUGH:

I don't say it though I
have the appetite.
I grin at your dinner plate,
ask "more?"
watching my manners, and the crack
that spreads under the gravy smear.

The battleship is listing
on t.v. in a movie I was taught to love:
one must learn to
stand for something of value.
Like Love or Battle.
And so my
being here with you, Love.
I am good at battle, clattering
like my pots and pans,
I am good
at standing for Love: I never
say it.

I listen
to this apartment listing
dangerously in the night; listen
to the shift of furniture
in the next room, the discontent
of things trying to escape from drawers.
I lie next to you

compensating
like a sailor in rough weather.

I practice the word to myself, the one
I must say because
our shadows dismember
now in the dark. Break up
like a great ship. Because
I am going under, because nothing gives back
its dead. Because
you, pitching gently beside me,
do not want more.

AN IMPOSSIBLE COUCH TO REST ON

You are still in your resting position:
arms folded across your breathing.
The meticulous knot of your tie, undone.
The boat you wait for
hasn't arrived: there is
no boat.

I like to think
your mouth falls open because everything
falls open. Sleep releases you
as a hand would, having drained you.

Listen, Love, consider me
available as your pillow. There are
many pillows to sort through.
Think of them as air, you can breathe them forever,
they never go away, they expand
and breathe back on your face in bed.
When you turn out the light and touch them
they are dear faces you've loved all your life.

I'm thinking (watching you
roll over on the couch) how nice
it would be to say,
You are everything.
You aren't.
I'll climb through the wall of your flowering sleep,
bringing with me the landscape I
like to live in. I'll perfect
survival there, I'll live in accordance
with deadly possibilities. Soon your dream
won't even be yours.

Didn't you invite me

into your dream to set up housekeeping?
I've agreed to the terms: I practice
carefully with my thumb
opening and closing the lids of your eyes.
I sit like a nurse beside you
pretending to be
anyone's nightmare but my own.

My wisest friends say, Don't ask
landscape for love unless you're already
in love; don't ask for shelter
unless you understand
shelter is merciless the way it hugs you.

Waking in a strange room
the window is the floor.
If I rise on my elbows in bed,
I bump my head on a huge restless ceiling.
I'm likely to walk
into a closet instead of the next room,
instead of into myself.
And so on.

You know from somewhere in your sleep
that I won't sleep until
you wake to tell me you.
can't. Survival is simple:
today, no thanks to our efforts,
one of us
is likely to breathe.

BEYOND HEARING, TO BE ASKED IN

You stumble out to the night
taking the window with you, superb
in your cigarette and hard life back in the 20's.
It's so far from here to you on the lawn,
crumpled into your coat—I imagine
you dead each time. My arms
shoot toward you, they know the only help
for the dead: to be rolled over,
and though beyond hearing, to be asked in.

Come in. Above it all, late for dinner.
Perfect as nuggets
of ice and glass. This jagged bit of dark
is nothing big: an acquaintance
lived in so long we trust him.
Let's laugh like nothing happened,
let's yell from sleep "come on"
at each other, at the dark.

HAND HOLD

I call you because there is nothing to say
and I want weather to assume
the role of carefully chosen phrases:
wind slapped through
to the joints of the buildings today,
and we were that inevitable couple
walking in company with streetlights toward
nowhere in particular,
we were the words we have:

Are you cold, and do you want
to stop yet? All the time agreeing
on the unsaid Yes, stop, one can do so little
with a word like Star or Lover,
there is no word to signify each body
holding itself against wind
when it should collapse, or each hand
folding in on itself—
not to find the fist, but for simple warmth.

Now you walk late alone, coat tossed
to the sand at the lakeside where
something once promised to happen, something once
spread itself at your feet,
and only you would know it as more than water.
Tonight if you answered I
was going to tell you Autumn is my time:
things let go with sharp ease.
But you are not there, you hunch beside water
lost in the story of yourself,

and I would not know you, I would understand
only the roll of carefully chosen waves
as they enter your pockets.
In a month I would write, The moon
washes us away, though I know
Moon is too close to Star, Autumn too close to Lover.
For this language of letting go
we need words that mean to be silent
and to imply
an understanding better than our choices.
Inside such words how exceptional the story
might become: the two of us, wires
strung together across all this silence.

LOVE POEM

You turn away after dinner, enjoying
some start of memory you never tell me
except in pointing to the bench on the lawn:
how its shadow lingers . . .
perhaps your mother, perhaps her scarf, long
blown across your face.
Together you strode
out through glass doors, across winter grass,
her woolen hem ticking dry stubble,
and you sat with her,
centered on that great stone bench,
waiting with the patience of her waiting,
sensing she waited the approach
she could not speak of or think, but knew:
something more than the closing in
of the purple cold: some
impossible situation in the stars up there,
impossible as you or her, mother or son, and all
that breath fading off into hollow light.

I watch through the high window, you
standing beside that bench in snow,
staring down at its fine flat face as if
positioning, just so, that long-remembered

approach with no name, without even
a sound. You can't explain, and
that hopelessness of speech calms me.
I fancy myself, a moment, striding coatless
through the emptying light to stand
beside you. Instead, I turn
toward blue china dishes scattered like boats
on the checkered cloth.
Out there, your back hums
with the memory of mine here, turning in the window,
though you will never speak of it: I am
a newer recollection without words.
When you enter raw-faced, iced,
I won't turn from the table, but all of me
will turn.

WAKING

You bring me coffee. I don't
understand love, but accept it.
I lie against your waist because
that is like waking: what happens, true
as light.

The day may be unlike
a day, may be like steam: some revery
of possibility.
I accept it, because
you accept me, say I am lovely, and
mean it all purely as sleep.

I love sleep because it is
like you: rest, unfettered by senselessness.
I love the possibility
that nothing may happen, nothing at all.
That we may
go to bed early like bears, remembering nothing
but our dream: sap rising
in the trunks of maples, beginning
in sequence, in time.

for Neil Lukatch

GRAVITY

Autumn again: I am calm.
Leaves dangle, and I become
my life as I was taught to think it:
ice impending . . . yet
my nerve ends don't sense ice.
I move against the cycle, leap up,
not suspecting I've gone too far.

I visit my new boots upon
the colored leaves that were sidewalks,
imagining my cheek turned maple red.
I gaze in at windows:
the plants cut back, comforters placed
strategically on the arms of chairs.
Not so much is demanded now,
not so much
bare-armed, breast-shaking life. Thoughts go now
to pulling through.

And so it is my season, my turn, me
with my solid steps, my
hair grown unseemly long.
Me, some pioneer, some example unafraid
to stroll leisurely
onto early ice. If I were a mountain man
I'd grow a beard, wear raw skins.
Instead, once around the block,
I pick up some stray leaf, say nothing
of having thought it a hand, a companion

better than human. I carry it home,
watch it curl slowly in the corner of my bedroom.

If I were Autumn, I'd observe
how subtly drops the hair from the head, how
quickly are shed the words with which
one hangs on to a thought, and soon
little is left but this brilliant
canopy of color no thought could create.
If this is the season before ending, then
don't stop to talk if we should meet. Let
me be—calm here, thinner, settled down
in my boots with a thought: there cannot
be more than skeleton and root.

for Richard Lowenberg

COME INTO THE NIGHT GROVE

These cedars don't hear
the little tune I hum, they tune
to the shift of bone against skin,
skin against air as I enter
the grove. I have not planned
a return, I don't turn
back toward you, waiting certain
as daylight, as
business unfinished.

It would startle you
to note how little of my face is left.
Already the eyes
have scattered among high leaves.
And this fever that nested
so reasonably in the cheek walls
careens, drunk animal, does
what it wants.

My body walks on
through the grove without me
as if it had purpose, a place
to get to. I do not. I am here,
distilled to fine mist
that hangs in the branches.
I am this ring around the moon. I try
to tell you: weather. Do not
be caught in the open.

Come into the grove. I want
to settle my facelessness
against yours. I want to say

nothing, remember nothing,
though yes I know always
someone stands at the edge of trees,
resisting entrance and by that resistance
yanking us back
into our shoes for our own sakes.

Do you stare after me
suspecting my body is a shell, a machine?
Do your eyes squint toward
some imaginary point of dark
on the far side of the grove where you believe
memory must turn me back
toward you? Listen. I remember
nothing, I have become the trees.
If you will not enter, stand still
a new way: roots, not resistance.
I breathe at you, I am nodding. Won't
you breathe back?
What we let go of with every pore, is
what keeps us alive.

Carnegie-Mellon Poetry

The Living and the Dead,
  Ann Hayes (1975)

In the Face of Descent,
  T. Alan Broughton (1975)

The Week the Dirigible Came,
  Jay Meek (1976)

Full of Lust and Good Usage,
  Stephen Dunn (1976)

*How I Escaped from the Labyrinth and
    Other Poems,*
  Philip Dacey (1977)

The Lady from the Dark Green Hills,
  Jim Hall (1977)

For Luck: Poems 1962-1977,
  H. L. Van Brunt (1977)

By the Wreckmaster's Cottage,
  Paula Rankin (1977)

New & Selected Poems,
  James Bertolino (1978)

The Sun Fetcher,
  Michael Dennis Browne (1978)

A Circus of Needs,
  Stephen Dunn (1978)

The Crowd Inside,
  Elizabeth Libbey (1978)

Paying Back the Sea,
  Philip Dow (1979)